SCRIPT TITLE

Written by

Name of First Writer

Based on, If Any

Address
Phone Number

RACHEL-a screenplay

By K Kelly

Copyright ©2016

FICTITIOUS COUNTRY

EXT. SMALL FAMILY FARM -DAY

A man is carrying the last chicken away from the small enclosure.

MAN

Rachel, your father said for me to take a chicken.

Rachel is removing a note that reads, Final Notice, from the front door of the small family farm. With the note in hand, She waves to the man than climbs into an old truck and heads to PEL TOWN leaving the family farm in the distance behind her

INT. PEL STREET PUB - DAY (COND'T)

Rachel walks directly to the bar where her father is seated. A tall glass of beer and a rolled document are on the bar counter in front of him.

RACHEL

Father, did you walk to town?

FATHER

I left the truck for you, in case you wanted to go somewhere. I like to walk.

RACHEL

We have until the end of the week to pay. You realize we can't pay because you have given away just about all of our livestock.

FATHER

Since this civil uprising, everyone is having trouble putting food on the table. I feel bad, you left college to help with me with the farm.

RACHEL

I came back to make sure you are doing okay, with this unrest. What is that document?

FATHER

A man hear me tell the bartender about the farm being foreclosed and he said if I deliver this document for him that there will be enough money to stop the foreclosing. We need to take the truck

Two military police enter. They walk up to the table with the document on it.

INT. SMALL MILITARY COMPOUND-DAY

Rachel and her father wait inside a small room that has one chair and one desk. On the desk is a bottle of Gin and the document. Peter, in uniform, enters. He carries three shot glasses than pours a shot glass full of gin and drinks it down.

PETER

You were brought to my compound for questioning. Shots?

RACHEL

I prefer a glass of wine.

FATHER

You wouldn't even know her after she has liquor, a completely different person. I will have a shot.

PETER

The man you were talking to at the bar, is he your friend?

FATHER

He was giving me employment. I am to deliver this document for him. All his Family were puking his guts out with the flu. He must be a good man because he was in a hurry to get back to take care of them.

PETER

It sounds like you are a good friend.

Peter drinks another shot than pours one for Father.

FATHER

I don't know the man. I was delivering the document as a favor. Actually, he was doing me a favor.

PETER

Where did you two come from?

RACHEL

We have a family farm.

PETER

Good people and hard workers come from the farm.

RACHEL

That's us.

PETER

Before the uprising, I was a financial consultant with Beck's Financial Center. Work That I am returning to soon.

RACHEL

It is a beautiful building.

PETER

Beck's is the 'Top' financial investment firm in this city.

RACHEL

Peter, take the document, father doesn't want to deliver something that he shouldn't be.

Peter picks up the document handing it to Rachel's Father.

PETER

Take it and leave. Make a little money for yourself. Only The uprising will probably end before you collect.

RACHEL

You said this document is military.

Peter

The treatise is being signed as we talk. This document is a useless piece of paper, but you said you will be paid to deliver it-Go ahead. I would like to see you again.

RACHEL

How?

PETER

Call me at Beck's Financial Center. I am a financial adviser, not a soldier.

RACHEL

Okay.

PETER

Soon.

FATHER

Peter, you say it is okay to do. I believe you. My daughter
and I will deliver it. Could someone, please, give us a ride
back to our truck?

Peter nods, yes, as his eyes gaze at Rachel.

DISSOLVE TO: winding road TO THE HILLS:

EXT. WINDING ROAD TO THE HILLS-MORNING

Rachel and her father drive the old truck up a slanted rocky
road.

EXT. SHANKS MOTEL-DAY

Once in town, they take the document to the hotel and collect
a large envelope of money.

EXT. BANK-NIGHT (COND'T)

Rachel and her father go into the bank. They pay the
delinquent payment.

SEVERAL MONTHS LATER:

INT./EXT. FAMILY FARM-DAY

Outside, the animal pens are full. Inside, Father is reading
the newspaper. He and Rachel are dressed to go out. They are
meeting Peter.

RACHEL

Are you ready?

I have been ready for an hour already. I feel shaky.

RACHEL

It is probably nerves. We only met Peter once. I am alitlle
nervous too.

FATHER

He tried to do a nice thing for us, but the uprising didn't
end as soon as he predicted.

RACHEL

It is over now. You did nothing wrong. Peter said so. When we
get to town and have a nice meal with Peter-You will feel
better. Peter will tell you there is nothing for you to be
upset about.

PEL TOWN

FICTITIOUS COUNTRY COND'T

THE TOWN OF PEL

INT. RESTAURANT DAY (COND'T)

Peter, Rachel and her father are dining. Father is sweating
and hasn't eaten a bite.

RACHEL

Peter, please reassure my father. He thinks it was wrong to
deliver the document.

PETER

It was fine. Don't worry.

FATHER

Did you read that document?

PETER

It doesn't matter.

FATHER

I read in the newspaper that the bridge named on the document was blown up a week after we delivered it. I feel responsible.

PETER

The uprising is over. Forget about it.

FATHER LOOKS ILL. HE IS SWEATING PROFUSELY AND HE CAN'T CATCH HIS BREATH.

INT. HOSPITAL-DAY (COND'T)

 The Doctor, Gerald Ludwich, shines A small light shines into her father's eyes. Rachel and Peter are near father's bed.

DOCTOR GERALD LUDWICH

(TO RACHEL)

I am doctor Ludwich. Your father has suffered a major heart attack. We Are trying to get him stabilized.

PETER

Rachel, I live close to the hospital. You Can stay at my place. I'll sleep on the couch. You can have my bedroom.

RACHEL

I am not leaving father. I'll drive to the farm and get a change of clothes; feed the animals and ask the neighbors if they would take care of the farm while we are gone. They Love dad.

PETER

I'll come by the hospital to visit.

INT. HOSPITAL DAY COND'T

Rachel has slept in a chair next. To her father's hospital bed. Peter has stopped by.

RACHEL

He worsened overnight.

PETER

I will stay with you.

A Priest enters the room and performs the last rights; anointing Father's forehead with oil. Soon after, all vital signs stop.

RACHEL

I am not going back to the farm without father.

INT. PETER'S CONDOMINIUM- DAY

KITCHEN TABLE

Rachel is staying with Peter. He sleeps on the couch and she in his bedroom. They are eating breakfast.

PETER

There is an opening at the switchboard at Becks. I suggested you for the position.

RACHEL

The farm sold three weeks after father was buried. I am ready for a new beginning. Thank You, Peter, for all of your help and for letting me have the bedroom. None of this was your doing. Father Was not well. The Farm was always on the blink of foreclosure. It was stressful for him.

Establishing shot PEL STREET

A few tall buildings and many small buildings line Pel Street. The two largest and best designed buildings are the Becks Financial Center and The University.

The streets are alive with vendors and artists.

INT. PETER'S CONDOMINIUM - NIGHT

A FEW WEEKS LATER

Rachel lies on the couch with her bare feet hung over the arm. She is exhausted. Peter is sitting in the chair next to her.

PETER

I thought you were a strong farm girl.

RACHEL

I'll get used to the Switchboard.

PETER

You could start getting used to me.

PETER LEANS TO KISS HER.

RACHEL

The couch is fine for me. Please, take your bedroom back. I am saving for a place. I was under the impression that we were friends.

Peter stands, forgoing the kiss. He carries a bottle of gin with him to his bedroom.

INT. PETER'S CONDOMINIUM - NIGHT DAYS LATER

LIVING ROOM

Rachel is sweeping the living room. Peter opens the door and staggers through. His Tie is ruffled and his suit is mussed and wrinkled as is his hair. Peter Holds his arms out to Rachel. She Steps away from his grasp.

PETER

I love you.

RACHEL

I like you.

ESTABLISHING SHOT

Beck's Financial Center across from which is a deli.

INT. BECK'S FINANCIAL CENTER- DAY

SWITCHBOARD

Rachel, wearing a headset, is busy at the switchboard as
Peter stands near, talking to her regardless that Rachel is
still working. Beside him is a short bald man-Charles Beck.

PETER

Rachel It is time for lunch. This is Mr. Beck. The big shot
himself and my best friend. He is usually right about
everything. He gives great advice.

(TO MR. BECK)

Charles, this is the love of my life, my life itself; the one
and only-Rachel.

MR. BECK

You can see why Peter is my number one salesman.

Rachel is still taking calls, but watches Peter and Mr. Beck.
Heather, Mr. Beck's only child, walks over to switchboard.

HEATHER

Number one salesman-You must be talking about John. He was
the best, but I don't think we'll get him back here, Daddy.
He is forever committed to his passion establishing funds for
endangered species. But I am trying.

HEATHER TURNS AND LOOKS AT RACHEL.

MR.BECK

Heather, Peter is back. I was talking about him, this time.

Rachel takes off her headset and holds it out to Heather.
With A disbelieving look upon her face Heather takes the
headset and immediately becomes busy.

INT. DELI-DAY

(COND'T)

Peter and Mr. Beck are emerged in conversation. Rachel has
finished her lunch and sits completely complacent.

MR. BECK

Peter, just send him to my office. That stock has shown good
past performance.

PETER

Charles ,that is what I told him about this stock. I think he
should include it in his portfolio.

RACHEL

Peter, I am finished. See you later.

Peter, unexpectedly, kisses Rachel before she stands to
leave.

INT. BECK'S FINANCIAL CENTER - DAY (COND'T)

Rachel flicks the answering machine switch to on, relieving
Heather.

HEATHER

Don't do that to me again. I didn't know where the hold
switch was. Now, I really do know part of this business.

RACHEL

Sorry, I thought you came over to relieve me for lunch. Peter and I are just friends.

HEATHER

Mr. Beck is my father. My name is Heather. I wanted to ask you about my shirt. I had to get a new outfit to go out with John. I think we are flying somewhere. I mean what do you wear to go out with a pilot?

RACHEL

I dated a crop duster pilot. I don't remember what I wore.

HEATHER

I few on the jumbo jet he piloted to Paris where I than chose an outfit and a fur.

RACHEL

John?

HEATHER

No. My John does fly small planes but he is into fund raising for endangered animals. I wouldn't wear a real fur around him. John is boring; however, he does throw the most extravagant jollifications; not the cake and ice cream socials that, I am sure, you are custom to.

RACHEL

Interesting.

HEATHER

John is picking me up after work this evening. Please, come and meet him. I want you to see his car.

RACHEL

Okay, but I need to get back to work.

HEATHER REACHES OVER AND FLICKS THE SWITCH ON THE SWITCHBOARD.

HEATHER

I got it.

INT. FINANCIAL CENTER -NIGHT (COND'T)

Peter stops by the switchboard to get Rachel as the work day is finished.

PETER

Are you ready to go home?

RACHEL

No. I'll be 'home' later. Heather, Mr. Beck's daughter wants to show me something.

PETER

I'd like to show you something tonight.

RACHEL

Peter!

PETER

You didn't resist that kiss at lunch.

RACHEL

I didn't have time to.

PETER

I'll be waiting to hear that old truck of yours pull up.

Later

Rachel and Heather stand outside of the financial center as a red sports car pulls up swiftly in front of them.

Through the open car's door, Rachel sees John's handsome face.

(ANGLE ON)

We see Rachel's awe at the sight of John's good looks. We see that Rachel is love struck. Heather notices Rachel's stunned expression.

HEATHER

That's right. Let's go for drinks. Ride with us. John-who always stays sober- will take us home. I am

so dry. What A day I have had. Daddy with his negative comments. Daddy saying he wants John back-He could run this business. Heather just runs around. It makes me mad. He just fuels me and makes me want to achieve more.

(DISSOLVE)

INT. PETER'S CONDOMINIUM - day (COND'T)

LIVING ROOM

Peter is pacing back and forth with an alcoholic drink in his hand. Rachel just arrives home.

PETER

I thought that old truck of yours broke down or something happened to you.

RACHEL

I made a friend.

PETER

You should have called. I left several messages on your phone.

RACHEL

I should have called. Did you need anything?

Peter hugs Rachel than picks her up and lays her on the couch.

PETER

I need you

RACHEL

Stop. I thought we were friends. I don't feel that way about you.

PETER STANDS- HE STAGGERS AWAY.

INT. BECK'S FINANCIAL CENTER-DAY

Rachel is at the switchboard. Heather has just arrived at work.

RACHEL

Heather, Peter and I are not getting along. Do you know a place where I can stay? I just begun working at the financial center I don't want to go in debt. That is what my father did with the farm. When I sold the farm quickly at a low price, than paid off loans father owed. It didn't leave a profit.

HEATHER

Do not spend more that you have. That is firm financial advice from an expert-me. I have an extra room I will rent to you, cheap.

Peter and Mr. Beck stop by the switchboard as they head to lunch.

RACHEL

Peter, instead of lunch today, I thought I would do some shopping.

INT. RED SPORTS CAR DAY (COND'T)

LUNCH

Heather is driving Rachel to Peter's condo.

RACHEL

John has such a nice sports car.

HEATHER

This car is mine. John and I picked our cars out together for one of our dates.

RACHEL

It sounds like love.

HEATHER

I am thinking about the financial center constantly. I think I am in love with it. If I could get him to come back to work would mean big money. Clients like him.

INT./EXT. PETER'S CONDOMINIUM - DAY (COND'T)

At the kitchen table, Rachel writes a letter. Heather is carrying Rachel's suitcases out the door.

Angle on letter

Peter, thank you for your support after my father died. I cannot give you more than friendship. Good-bye. Rachel.

EXT. PETER'S CONDOMINIUM -DAY

Rachel's old truck is packed.

HEATHER

Couldn't you leave that truck?

THE TRUCK WON'T START.

Rachel

I will have to, it won't start.

HEATHER

Leave it. Sign the title over to him.

HEATHER CARRIES A SUITCASE FROM THE OLD TRUCK TO HER RED SPORTS CAR.

RACHEL

Okay.

Rachel takes the title and a pen from the glove compartment.

DISSOLVE:

MOVING:

Heather's red sports car going toward the ocean.

ANGLE ON

HEATHER'S RED SPORTS CAR PASSES BETWEEN TWO LARGE GATES. THIS IS THE ENTRANCE TO THE BEACH FRONT

COMMUNITY CONSISTING OF ELABORATE BEACH HOUSES.

EXT. BEACH FRONT COMMUNITY-DAY

Rachel follows Heather as each carry a suitcase to Heather's large beach house. The green-blue hue of

the ocean is behind them.

HEATHER

John's beach house is three houses down from mine.

RACHEL

You can see him any time you want.

Rachel and Heather go inside the large beach house.

HEATHER

John works at home, so that is literally true.

EXT. BECK'S FINANCIAL CENTER-DAY

Peter and Mr. Beck are walking and talking.

MR. BECK

You have been skipping lunch. You have to eat sooner or later, Peter.

PETER

Charles, I haven't been hungry since Rachel left. I imagined my life with her. I can't imagine my life without her. The future seems nothingness.

MR. BECK

It only seems that way now. You don't know the future.

INT. HEATHER'S RED SPORTS CAR-NIGHT

HEATHER PULLS HER RED SPORTS CAR ONTO THE SIDE OF THE ROAD.

HEATHER

Peter is behind us and he waved for me to pull over.

Maybe he wants to tell me something about my car-a broken
taillight or low tire though I don't see any dash lights on.

WIDER ANGLE

The pursing car stops; it touches the bumper of the red
sports car.

ANGLE ON

Peter approaches the passenger side here Rachel is sitting
stiffly straight.

PETER

I got your note. I don't need a friend. I will get the truck
towed to the junk yard for you.

FOLLOW

Peter walks slowly back to his car, his head hung low. Before
opening the car door, Peter changes disposition, lifting his
head high.

EXT. HEATHER'S BEACH HOUSE-NIGHT

BEACH

FOLLOW

RACHEL AND HEATHER EACH HAVE AN END TO A LARGE WICKER BASKET
CONTAINING A BOTTLE OF VODKA. HEATHER ACTS SILLY, GIGGLING
AND LAUGHING, AS SHE CARRIES HER END. AFTER THIRTEEN STEPS,
THEY STOP, OPEN THE WICKER BASKET, REMOVE TWO GLASSES AND
TAKE A SHOT. THEY LAUGH, DRINK THAN CONTINUE THE JOURNEY WITH
THE BASKET.

THE WEATHER IS WINDY; THE SKY STORMY AND THE OCEAN WATER
CHOPPY. IT IS SPRINKLING LIGHT RAIN ON THE BEACH.

RACHEL

This is a liquor occasion.

I thought John doesn't drink.

HEATHER

He doesn't, but I am going to get him drunk.

RACHEL

Why?

HEATHER

Because he's boring. I can only stand being around him if I can get him drunk.

RACHEL

He seems to be kind and intelligent.

EXT. JOHN'S BEACH HOUSE (COND'T)

RACHEL AND HEATHER SET THE BASKET ONTO THE SAND. THE SEA-GRASS IS BEING BLOWN BY THE STRONG GUSTS OF WIND.

FOLLOW

HEATHER GOES UP JOHN'S FRONT PORCH STEPS.

HEATHER GIGGLES AS SHE RINGS THE DOORBELL. JOHN COMES OUT. HEATHER NEARLY FALLS BACKWARDS DOWN THE STEPS. JOHN STEADIES HER WITH BOTH HIS ARMS WHICH HE THAN WRAPS THEM AROUND HER.

ANGLE ON

Rachel's expression of disapproval.

EXT. BEACH FRONT (COND'T)

JOHN, HEATHER, AND RACHEL SIT TAKING SHOTS. HEATHER GIGGLES
NON-STOP AND SHE FILLS JOHN'S GLASS, REPEATEDLY.

JOHN

I have something for you.

JOHN TAKES A RING OUT OF HIS POCKET; HE PUTS IT ON HEATHER'S
OUTSTRETCHED FINGER. RACHEL STANDS.

FOLLOW

RACHEL WALKS BACK TO HEATHER'S BEACH HOUSE.

INT./EXT. HEATHER'S BEACH HOUSE (LATER)

LIVING ROOM

Heather is asleep on the couch. Rachel is laying on the
floor. Blankets sprawled about.

RACHEL

I am going to check on John. He doesn't drink, but he drank a
lot.

HEATHER IS SOUND ASLEEP. RACHEL'S FIRST ATTEMPT TO GO OUTSIDE
LANDS HER IN ANOTHER ROOM OF THE HOUSE FOR

SHE IS INTOXICATED. FINALLY, SHE LEAVES WEARING HER NIGHT
GOWN.

EXT. BEACH FRONT (COND'T)

THE WIND HOWLS O.S

FOLLOW

THE BREEZE HAS TURNED TO A VIOLENT WIND THAT SENDS LARGE SWELLS CRASHING TO THE SHORE. THE RAIN FALLS HEAVILY. RACHEL WALKS BARE FOOT THROUGH THE SAND AND THE STORM, TOWARDS JOHN'S BEACH HOUSE.

INT/EXT JOHN'S BEACH HOUSE (COND'T)

PORCH

RACHEL REPEATEDLY BANGS ON JOHN'S BEACH HOUSE DOOR, AND RINGS THE DOORBELL, TO NO AVAIL. SEVERAL MINUTES PASS THAN THE DOOR OPENS EXPOSING JOHN'S MUSCULAR STATUE STANDING WITHIN THE DOOR FRAME.

JOHN

You are soaking wet, come inside. Is anything wrong?

RACHEL

I want to know why? I mean-I came to check on you. You seem okay.

JOHN

Yes. What do you mean why?

RACHEL

Why marry Heather?

JOHN IS STUMBLING AND SLURRING HIS WORDS. HE IS INTOXICATED.

JOHN

Charles is my best friend. Heather is his daughter and she's great. Right.

RACHEL

She is? She's nice.

JOHN

You are shivering.

JOHN THROWS A LOG INTO THE FIREPLACE BUT IS TOO DRUNK TO FIND THE MATCHES.

JOHN

Come to the kitchen, warm yourself by the stove.

KITCHEN

John is drunk and lusty as he watches Rachel warm herself by the stove. They consummate after which John seems to quickly sober up.

JOHN

I am marrying Heather. I am sorry.

RACHEL

I assumed that you wanted to. It didn't sink in that it was real between you and Heather, until now.

EXT. BEACH FRONT (COND'T)

RACHEL WALKS SLOWLY AND WISTFULLY ALONG THE SAND TOWARDS
HEATHER'S BEACH HOUSE. SHE NOTICES A LONE SEAGULL PERCHED ON
A PIER; BEYOND, WHICH IS A RAINBOW.

INT. BECK'S FINANCIAL CENTER-DAY

SWITCHBOARD

Rachel walks into work and notices that there is a new
switchboard operator.

RACHEL

Who are you?

NEW SWITCHBOARD OPERATOR

I am the new operator.

FOLLOW

RACHEL WALKS THROUGH THE HALL PAST SEVERAL CUBICLES,
CONTINUING TOA DOOR MARKED WITH MR. BECK'S

NAMEPLATE. SHE ENTERS WITHOUT KNOCKING.

INT. MR. BECK'S OFFICE - DAY

Mr. Beck is writing. He won't look at Rachel.

MR. BECK

You're fired.

RACHEL

Why? I need this job.

MR.BECK

Bad performance.

RACHEL

Mr. Beck, what have I ever done to you?

MR. BECK

It is not what you did to me.

Rachel leaves the office, she shuts the door hard.

INT. HALLWAY (COND'T)

Upset, Rachel bumps into Heather.

RACHEL

Your father fired me. Talk to him. Tell him that he can't do
that.

HEATHER

Daddy won't listen to me. We'll talk to my mother.

EXT SHOT

A beautiful mansion. The home belongs to Mr. And Mrs. Beck.

INT. MANSION - DAY

KITCHEN

HEATHER IS IN THE KITCHEN STUFFING HER FACE WITH FOOD FROM
HER MOTHER'S REFRIGERATOR WHILE RACHEL AND THE HOUSEKEEPER
WATCH.

RACHEL

Heather, how can you eat when I am unemployed?

Housekeeper

Heather, you still eat like when you were a little girl and
you still make a mess.

MRS. BECK ENTERS. SHE HAS A WIDE EYED INNOCENCE AND CHILDLIKE
QUALITIES ABOUT. SHE RAMBLES ON TALKING AS NON-STOP AS HER
DAUGHTER.

MRS. BECK

Everybody from my tea club is gone now. Please, come in and
sit down. And, goody-goody, we have more tea left.

LIVING ROOM (COND'T)

The three ladies converse.

HEATHER

Mommy, this is Rachel. She is the girl sharing my beach house
with me.

MRS. BECK

Goody, now you are not alone in that big beach house. I told
your daddy, what is that little girl going to do in that big
beach house? He said, she won't be alone when John and she
are married. He wants you to marry John so badly.

HEATHER

John did ask me to marry him; as I remember. He is renting out his beach house, so we'll be living in mine.

RACHEL

Please, we were talking about me. What am I going to do? Your husband fired me. He is so inconsiderate. I need a life.

MRS.BECK

Rachel, dear, Mr. Becks is great at talking, but not at listening.

The housekeeper enters with more tea.

HOUSEKEEPER

More tea?

HEATHER

Yes, and lots more sugar in the sugar pot. We are celebrating.

RACHEL

No-thank you.

MRS. BECK

Not I. Thank you. Does tomorrow begin your week off, already?

HOUSEKEEPER

It does. I hate to leave you without anybody.

MRS. BECK

Rachel, why don't you take the place of our other housekeeper who quit? She worked one week on-living here than a week off. Would that work for you?

RACHEL

Yes, it would. I'll have more tea now.

HEATHER

On your weeks off, Rachel, you can still stay at my beach house.

WEEKS LATER

INT. Mansion - DAY

Rachel is finishing setting the table with breakfast eggs, bacon, toast and a large pitcher of orange juice. The Becks are seated at the table. Mr. Becks has begun to eat his eggs.

MR. BECK

These eggs have no flavor.

MRS. BECK

Mine are fine.

RACHEL

Mr. Beck, would you like something else?

MR. BECK

Fix something decent.

Ms. Beck giggles as she and her husband stand to leave the table and go upstairs.

LIVING ROOM (COND'T)

LATER

Rachel is heaving a vacuum cleaner up the stairs. We see the stairs as she now comes back down and the living room door shuts as Mr. Beck has just left the room. Rachel is shocked to see dirt from a potted plant spewed on the freshly cleaned carpet.

EXT. RED SPORTS CAR DAY (COND'T)

HEATHER IS SITTING IN THE DRIVER'S SEAT, AS RACHEL THROWS HER ONE SUITCASE INTO THE BACK. THEY DRIVE HOME. THERE IS A SHOPPING BAG IN THE BACK SEAT.

RACHEL

This week has been hell. Your father is so mean to me.

HEATHER

Mother and I are planning the wedding. Look in shopping bag.

Rachel takes a black dress out of the shopping bag.

RACHEL

It is beautiful.

HEATHER

That is the dress I am wearing on John and mine's honeymoon night. Now, you need a bridesmaid's dress because I need a bridesmaid.

RACHEL

I don't feel in shape as when I worked on the farm- and no, housework is not the same as farm work.

HEATHER

My spa will fix you.

RACHEL

I wish it could fix your father.

EXT. Spa - DAY

OUTDOOR TRACK

Dressed in exercise clothes, Rachel and Heather run on an outdoor track.

HOT SPRINGS

Heather is up to her shoulders in bubbling, steaming water. Rachel sits on the side with her feet dangling in.

HEATHER

Why aren't you getting in.

RACHEL

Because. I read somewhere that hot water isn't good to be in if your pregnant. Heather, I got with John.

HEATHER

The John I know?

RACHEL

Yes.

HEATHER

But, he's marrying me.

RACHEL

Yes.

HEATHER

Not you.

RACHEL

Yes.

HEATHER

He is marrying me. Isn't that ironic.

INT. BRIDAL SHOP - DAY

Heather and Rachel are among beautiful wedding gowns and various dresses.

HEATHER

Rachel, I chose pink for the bridesmaid's gown. Try on these three pink gowns. I am not sure which I like best.

RACHEL

I can't be your bridesmaid, now.

HEATHER

Rachel, I set goals and I have goals set for me, so I am
plenty busy. I keep focused on them and I don't get
sidetracked. I am getting married. That is what matters now-
Not you- or your pregnancy.

RACHEL

I didn't think that you would want me around.

HEATHER

John and I talk about everything. He actually already told me
about the baby. We want yo to live with us on the weeks you
don't work at my parents.

RACHEL

Really?

HEATHER

John and I want you and the baby to stay with us. We plan to
give this baby a good life.

INT. MANSION - DAY

KITCHEN

RACHEL IS BACK AT WORK IN THE BECK'S MANSION WHERE SHE IS
LOADING THE DISHWASHER. MR. BECK ENTERS THE KITCHEN AND
PURPOSELY DROPS A DISH. RACHEL WATCHES IT SHATTER. SHE
WHISPERS TO HERSELF.

RACHEL

Another week in hell.

THE WEDDING
INT. CHURCH - DAY

JOHN AND HEATHER'S WEDDING CEREMONY IS BEGINNING.

BRIDAL DRESSING ROOM

HEATHER IS DRESSED IN HER WHITE GOWN AND RACHEL IN HER PINK
BRIDESMAID'S DRESS. THEY STRAIGHTEN THEIR HAIR ONE LAST TIME.
MR.BECK STAGGERS THROUGH THE DOOR, DRINK IN HAND.

MR. BECK

My fifth drink. Now, I am ready to walk my only daughter down
the aisle.

HEATHER

Rachel, you can ride home with my father. He is taking my car
home after the wedding.

EXT. RED SPORTS CAR DAY (COND'T)

BEACH FRONT COMMUNITY-

The curves of the road leading down to the Beach Front
Community is hazardous. Mr. Beck is intoxicated and driving
at an excessive speed. Heather's Red Sports Car skids around
the curves on the way to the Ocean front community than
careens over the steep rocky slope. The red sports car has
come to a stop. Mr. Beck is unconscious. Rachel looks at
Charles. Then she sees flames. The car is on fire.

Rachel unfastens her seat belt and Mr. Beck's. She unlocks
his door than pushes him out onto the ground before sliding
across the seat and out the driver's door. She crawls over
Mr. Beck than pulls him away from the wreckage.

INT. HOSPITAL ROOM - DAY

RACHEL AND MRS. BECK ARE STANDING NEXT TO MR. BECK WHO IS
GROGGY BUT AWAKE IN HIS HOSPITAL BED. DOCTOR GERALD LUDWICH,
MR. BECK'S DOCTOR, WALKS IN.

[TO RACHEL)

Thank you, Rachel, for saving my life.

DOCTOR GERALD LUDWICH

He has a concussion and will need to stay here for a few
days. I expect he'll make a full recovery. You Have my
respect. Rachel.

RACHEL

 You were my father's doctor.

DOCTOR GERALD LUDWICH

You do look familiar.

MRS. BECK

Doctor Ludwich, as you know, I chair many of the hospital's
committees. I am going to personally see that the hospital
throws you the biggest retirement party when you retire. Ten
months right, I'll mark my calendar.

DOCTOR GERALD LUDWICH

I am ready for it.

NINE MONTS LATER:

INT./EXT. HEATHER'S BEACH HOUSE-DAY

RACHEL WALKS ALONG THE BEACH INHALING DEEPLY THE SEA BREEZE. SHE SEES A SEAGULL PERCHED ON A PIER. SUDDENLY SHE HOLDS HER STOMACH AND HURRIES IN PAIN BACK TO THE BEACH HOUSE. JOHN IS TALKING ON HIS CELLPHONE.

JOHN

Their numbers are decreasing around the world. Thank you for your concern and much needed support.

RACHEL

My water broke.

SOME TIME LATER:

HOSPITAL RETIREMENT PARTY FOR DOCTOR GERALD LUDWICH

ANGLE ON

A banner reads- Congratulations-Doctor Ludwich. String music plays. Couples dance. Rachel is inside holding her newborn baby, Elizabeth.

GERALD

Congratulations to you and your husband.

RACHEL

Thank you, but there is no husband, or boyfriend for me. But Elizabeth's father adores her.

MRS. BECK APPROACHES.

MRS. BECK

Let me hold Elizabeth. You two dance.

GERALAD

Mrs. Beck is always trying to fix me up.

MRS. BECK

Consider yourself fixed.

GERALD AND RACHEL DANCE. THERE IS A SPECIAL CHEMISTRY BETWEEN THEM. A ROMANCE HAS BEGUN.

SERIES OF SHOTS OF GERALD AND RACHEL DATING; DINING; DANCING; WALKING-DATING.

INT./EXT. LITTLE RESTAURANT-DAY

GERALD SEATS HIMSELF ACROSS FROM RACHEL WHO IS BITING HER FINGERNAIL. A WAITER APPROACHES.

WAITER

May I take your order?

GERALD

A glass of milk, please.

RACHEL

I'll have the day's special.

THE WAITER LEAVES. GERALD PUTS HIS FIST TO HIS STOMACH AND PRESSES HARD.

RACHEL

Are you ill?

GERALD

I need the milk to sooth my ulcer. Why are you biting your fingernail?

RACHEL

I love to see Elizabeth with her father. I know how important mine was to me. He raised me alone. I can't stay with Heather and John forever.

GERALD

John can visit Elizabeth.

RACHEL

John rushes to her crib the minute he hears he is awake in the morning. He rocks her to sleep at night. He is a good father. When I move out, Elizabeth can stay with John and Heather-but I will still see Elizabeth and I will always will be her mother. Do you have children?

GERALD

A son. He's in college now. When my wife ran off, I was left to finish raising him. After lunch, I want you to meet someone important.

INT. ORPHANAGE - DAY

GERALD WALKS DELIBERATELY THROUGH THE HALLS, RACHEL WALKS BESIDE HIM. THEY ENTER A ROOM IN WHICH THERE ARE BABY CRIBS LINED AGAINST THE WALL. GERALD CONTINUES TO WALK TO THE CRIB WHICH HAS THE LOUDEST CRYING BABY. HE IS TAKING RACHEL TO MEET SHEILA.

GERALD

THIS WAS MY LAST PATIENT-SHEILA. THE STAFF LET ME NAME HER.
WE DIDN'T THINK SHEILA WAS GOING TO LIVE. SHEILA'S MOTHER
TRIED TO SELF -ABORT.

BABY SHEILA LOOKS UP WITH RECOGNITION AT GERALD AND REACHES
OUT HER HANDS.

RACHEL

You bonded with her.

GERALD

I visit weekly. I want Sheila to have a good home-would adopt
her myself. I understand how you feel about Elizabeth and her
father. I want Sheila to have a mother. My wife was a
wonderful mother. I loved to watch her with our son.

RACHEL GETS DOWN ON ONE KNEE AND SPEAKS ABOVE THE LOUD
CONTINUED CRYING.

RACHEL

We can give Sheila a family. Will you marry me?

GERALD TAKES RACHEL'S HAND, AND LIFTS HER TO STANDING. HE
PLACES SHEILA IN HER ARMS THAN HE KNEELS ON ONE KNEE.

GERALD

I fell in love with you the first time that I saw you. Would
you do me the honor of marrying me?

RACHEL

Yes.

AFTER GERALD'S AND RACHEL'S WEDDING:

EXT. GERALD AND RACHEL'S VILLA- DAY

Rachel is in labor. Gerald is carrying Rachel's overnight
bag. Rachel places Sheila into the arms of Ms. Wait.

RACHEL

I've been in labor since midnight. Thank you, Ms. Wait for
taking care of Sheila for us.

MS. WAIT

Drive Carefully.

GERALD

Definitely.

RACHEL

You are a good neighbor and a good friend.

MS. WAIT

Sheila is crying. I think she misses you already. I hope that
baby comes fast.

LATER

WHEN THEY PICK SHEILA UP FROM MS. WAIT'S

MS. WAIT

She cried the whole time you were gone.

TWO YEARS LATER:

INT. SHEILA'S DOCTOR'S OFFICE (FICTIOUS COUNTRY)- DAY

SHEILA IS TWO YEARS OLD. RACHEL HOLDS SHEILA WHO IS NOT TWO YEARS OLD.

(CRYING)

RACHEL (TO SHEILA'S DOCTOR)

She never sleeps more than twenty minutes and she clutches at her head and cries.

RACHEL HAS CIRCLES UNDER HER EYES FROM LACK OF SLEEP.

SHEILA'S DOCTOR

Sheila's had traumatic birth. Be patient with her. Give Sheila all the attention and love you can.

TWO YEARS LATER:

INT. Villa-night

BEDROOM

RACHEL AND GERALD ARE DRESSED FOR BED. SHEILA, FOUR YEARS OLD, IS IN THE MIDDLE OF THEIR BED. SHE HAS BEEN NON STOP CRYING FOR HOURS.

GERALD

Let's try rubbing her feet.

RACHEL

I've fed her, bathed her, and changed her. Massage is soothing.

GERALD

She is going to have to take the pain medication again. It'll help for awhile.

RACHEL

She's just a baby.

GERALD
She is a baby in chronic pain. Her doctor will have to prescribe something stronger.

INT. VILLA - DAY

KITCHEN

PANS ARE STEAMING ON THE STOVE. RACHEL CHOPS ONIONS. THERE IS A BABY GATE ACROSS THE ENTRANCE OF THE KITCHEN. SHEILA IS CRYING AT THE GATE.

RACHEL

Please, stop. I am trying to make dinner.

(CRYING)

(FOLLOW)

RACHEL TO THE GATE.

RACHEL

Lets try to get you to feel better so you can eat dinner with us.

Rachel picks Sheila up patting her back which makes Sheila cry louder. Rachel puts Sheila back down on the other side of the baby gate. Raina, walks over to the gate, she hand her mother a picture of a sailboat that she has drawn.

RACHEL LOOKS AT THE PICTURE FOR AWHILE. SHE SMILES.

RACHEL

Thank you, Raina. When I look at your picture, I feel like I am on a wonderful vacation.

RAINA SMILES.

TEN YEARS LATER:

EXT. VILLA-DAY

RAINA IS A TEENAGER. SHE IS IN THE FRONT YARD PAINTING A PICTURE.

(OS)

FROM THE VILA WE HEAR THE SOUNDS OF A DISTRESSED TEENAGE GIRL-SHEILA.

SHEILA

These headaches suck.

RACHEL

You need to work on choosing better words to express yourself. You are a strong girl.

RACHEL WALKS OUT OF THE HOUSE TO THE YARD. IN HER HANDS ARE CAR KEYS.

YARD

(RAINA'S POV)

RAINA SEES RACHEL WAVING HER OVER TO THE CAR. SHE RUNS OVER AND LOOKS INTO THE WINDOW AT RACHEL.

RACHEL

Run inside and put a dress on; brush your hair. Elizabeth graduated business college today.

RAINA

How come Elizabeth has never visited us?

RACHEL

I like visiting her.

INT. Car - DAY

RACHEL AND RAINA RIDE IN SILENCE.

RAINA

Mom, I need more red and yellow paint

RACHEL

Be quiet. Don't talk. I need silence.

INT./EXT. HEATHER'S BEACH HOUSE

(CONDT)

WHERE THEY HEAR JOHN AND HEATHERS' RAISED VOICES.

JOHN

I do work. Helping endangered species is my work. You wanted
to run the financial center. Isn't that why you married me,
so your father would let you?

HEATHER

I thought you would work more at the financial center. You
party while I work. Yet, you want to open a financial center
with your child. Isn't that the plan, but you won't help me;
after all I have done for you.

FRONT PORCH

ELIZABETH ANSWERS THE DOOR TO RACHEL AND RAINA. RACHEL
OVERHEARD HEATHER.

RACHEL

Elizabeth, how was your graduation ceremony? I am sorry that
we had to miss it.

ELIZABETH

It was good.

RACHEL

Let's take a walk.

BEACH FRONT

RACHEL WALKS ALONG THE OCEAN WITH HER TWO DAUGHTERS.
ELIZABETH DANCES ALONG BESIDE RACHEL. RAINA LAGS BEHIND AS
SHE STOPS TO LOOKS AT SEASHELLS.

RACHEL

Do they argue often?

ELIZABETH

Daddy bought a plane. He plans to spend the next two years flying around Tiger extinction awareness. Heather is an angry person.

RACHEL

She didn't use to be.

RAINA

(TO RACHEL AND ELIZABETH)

The seashells are beautiful.

RAINA CATCHES UP. SHE PLACES A SEASHELL IN EACH OF THEIR HANDS.

FOLLOW

JOHN PASSES RACHEL, RAINA, AND ELIZABETH BACK FROM THEIR WALK. HE IS CARRYING A SUITCASE TO HIS RED SPORTS CAR.

HEATHER SLAMS THE DOOR BEHIND HIM, NOT EVEN LOOKING AT ELIZABETH, RAINA, OR RACHEL.

HEATHER

(TO ELIZABETH)

I want you to live with your mother until you get on your feet. I will stay in touch.

John looks at Rachel as she shakes her head in agreement.
John gets into his Red Sports Car and drives away.

ELIZABETH

I need to get my things together. I'll come over tomorrow.

INT. VILLA - NIGHT

RACHEL'S/GERALD'S BEDROOM

RACHEL AND GERALD LAY AWAKE IN BED. GERALD RUBS HIS STOMACH
THAN DRINKS THE GLASS OF MILK HE KEEPS ON HIS NIGHT STAND.

HALLWAY

Sheila is hitting her head on the wall. Rachel goes into the
hall.

RACHEL

Why are you doing that? You are going to break the wall, or
your head.

Sheila

Hope it will be my head.

RACHEL

No sweetheart. Lets get you back to bed.

SHEILA WALKS AROUND IN A DREAM LIKE STATE, MEDICATED AND TIRED.

INT.VILLA - DAY

OS KNOCK AT DOOR

LIVING ROOM

Elizabeth is dressed impeccably and elegantly wearing a white dress with pink tights. Ribbons flow from her hair. She carries a suitcase. Rachel and Gerald greet her. Rachel Introduces Gerald

RACHEL

Gerald, meet my beautiful daughter.

GERAlD

I remember meeting Elizabeth-years ago. She was much shorter.

RACHEL

(Calling aloud)

Sheila. Raina.

RAINA EMERGES THE BEDROOM. SPOTS OF PAINT COVER HER CLOTHES.

SHEILA (OS)

I am in the kitchen.

RACHEL TAKES ELIZABETH BY THE HAND. THEY WALK TO THE KITCHEN.

I knew you were coming. I baked a chocolate cake, with
chocolate icing.

FOLLOW

DINING ROOM

SHEILA IN A DREAM LIKE STATE, MEDICATED AND TIRED, IS HOLDING
THE CAKE FOR ALL TO SEE WHEN THE PLATTER TURNS SIDEWAYS AND
THE CAKE FALLS TO THE FLOOR.

RACHEL (TO SHEILA)

It's okay sweetheart. Everything will be okay.

RACHEL PUTS HER ARMS AROUND SHEILA WHO JUST LOOKS AT THE
CHOCOLATE MOUND OF MESS ON THE FLOOR THAN CLOSES HER EYES.

(TIME HAS PASSED)

EXT. MS. WAIT'S VILLA - DAY

FLOWER GARDEN

MS. WAIT AND ELIZABETH ARE BENT DOWN WEEDING THE FLOWER
GARDEN. ELIZABETH IS A YOUNG ADULT. IN THE BACKGROUND IS
RAINA SITTING IN FRONT OF A LARGE EASEL WHILE GERALD AND
RACHEL RAKE THEIR YARD.

MS. WAIT

How are you doing?

ELIZABETH

I enjoy spending time with my Mother.

MS. WAIT

Your Mother loves her family.

A HANDSOME ELDERLY GENTLEMAN-GEORGE-CARRIES A POTTED PLANT
EMERGES FROM THE GREENHOUSE.

GEORGE

A beautiful plant for my new bride.

ELIZABETH HUGS MS. WAIT. RACHEL IS RAKING GRASS CLIPPINGS,
SHE SEES THAT SOMETHING HAS HAPPENED AS SHE OBSERVES THE
HUGGING AND SMILING TAKING PLACE IN MS. WAIT'S YARD.

RACHEL WALKS TO MS. WAIT'S YARD.

(LONG SHOT ELIZABETH MOUTHING THE WORD 'CONGRATULATIONS'.)

RACHEL HUGS MS. WAIL AND THAN SHE HUGS GEORGE. RACHEL THAN
WAVES FOR GERALD TO COME OVER.

EXT. FICTITIOUS JUNGLE - DAY

ESTABLISHING SHOT:

Thick jungle and mountainous area. A small clearing that is a
TOWN. FURTHER THROUGH THE JUNGLE IS A HIDDEN FENCED AREA.

(POV PLANE)

AS JOHN IS PILOTING A SMALL AIRCRAFT. HE IS LOOKING THROUGH
BINOCULARS AT SOMETHING BELOW.

JOHN

(TO HIMSELF)

I thought you were extinct.

(Os a loud band from the plane's engine)

INT. GERALD'S AND RACHEL'S VILLA - DAY

KITCHEN

RAINA AND GERALD ARE ADDING CREAM TO THEIR PREPARED TEA.
GERALD HEADS FOR THE SHELF WHERE HE REMOVES A TEA CUP. RAINA
EXITS TO THE BEDROOM WITH HER CUP OF TEA.

GERLAD

MS. Wait married George.

GERALD TURNS, HE LOOKS AT SHEILA WHO IS HOLDING HER HEAD IN
PAIN.

GERALAD

You have taken your medication. It isn't working.

GERALD FINISHES HIS CUP OF TEA. HE BURPS LEAVING HIS EMPTY
TEA CUP ON THE TABLE; HE GOES TO GET A FRESH GLASS FROM THE
CUPBOARD, THAN FILLS IT WITH MILK. GERALD DRINKS WHILE
HOLDING HIS STOMACH.

EXT./INT. Villa-- DAY

FROM THE MAILBOX, ELIZABETH TAKES A LETTER SHE HAD SENT TO
HER FATHER, JOHN-IT IS MARKED RETURN. SHE TAKES HER CELLPHONE
FROM HER POCKET AND LOOKS THROUGH IT-THERE ARE NO MESSAGES OR
MISSED PHONE CALLS FROM JOHN, HER FATHER.

LIVING ROOM

RACHEL IS TALKING ON THE PHONE. SENSING SOMETHING IS WRONG, ELIZABETH WAITS NERVOUSLY NEARBY.

RACHEL SETS THE PHONE DOWN. SHE IS UPSET.

RACHEL

Elizabeth, your father's plane crashed. He was far in the jungle, he can't be returned to us. I am sorry.

EXT. Ms. WAIT'S VILLA - DAY

YARD

(WIDE ANGLE)

A MOTORCYCLE PULLS INTO MRS. WAIT'S YARD. THE FRONT WHEEL OF THE MOTORCYCLE CRUSHES A RED DAILY

FLOWER. RED, AGE 23, IS MRS. WAIT'S GRANDSON- WALKS UP TO MRS. WAIT'S DOOR. HE RINGS THE BELL, KNOCKS, BUT THERE IS NO ANSWER.

(FOLLOW)

RED WALKS ACROSS THE YARD.

INT. GERALD'S AND RACHEL'S VILLA (COND'T)

RACHEL AND GERALD TALK WITH THE NEW STRANGER. SHEILA STANDS CLOSE TO RED. HER EYES AFFIXED TO HIS ROUGH BUT HANDSOME FACE.

RED

Hello. Have you seen the woman who lives her.

GERALAD

Ms. Wait and George live there. Are you her Grandson?

RED

Yes.

RACHEL

Your Grandmother has shown us many pictures of you.

RED

I ran away from home when I was a kid than lived with my Grandmother and Grandfather. I've been on the road. This is a surprise- me being here. Who is George.

GERALD

Your Grandmother re-married

RED

Married? Why in the hell did she do that?

RACHEL LOOKS MOMENTARILY AT GERALD IN DISBELIEF AT RED.

RACHEL

It's not because she is pregnant.

GERALAD

Red, where are you staying?

RED

I am staying at my Grandmothers.

SHEILA POINTS.

SHEILA

Your Grandmother is home now.

(CUT TO)

GEORGE AND MS. WAIT EACH ARE CARRYING A FLAT OF FLOWERS. RED
APPROACHES; HE GIVES GEORGE A ONCE OVER LOOK.

Ms. WAIT

George, this is my Grandson, Red.

RACHEL

This is my new Grandfather?

GEORGE

I consider myself old, but it is good to meet you.

Red

Yeah. Well. Grandma, I need to talk with you. I was planning
on staying in town. Said good-bye to the band. They wouldn't
let me do my own songs. So, I am going on my own. Do my
songs. Make my own damn way.

Ms. WAIT

Your room is still here.

INT. GERALD'S AND RACHEL'S VILLA - NIGHT

DINING ROOM

GERALD, RACHEL, ELIZABETH, RAINA, SHEILA ARE SITTING AT THE
DINNER TABLE.

(OS RED SHOUTING)

GERLAD

Elizabeth, please, close the window.

Elizabeth closes the window.

(OS DOORBELL RINGS)

Rachel answers the door to Ms. Wait. They talk.

Ms. WAIT

I hate to disturb your dinner.

RACHEL

What is happening?

Ms. WAIT

I mentioned the word marriage.

RACHEL

Come in.

DINNER TABLE (COND'T)

Ms. Wait sips a glass of red wine.

RACHEL

It is so rude of your Grandson to start an argument.

(Os doorbell)

(FOLLOW)

Sheila answers the door. Red walks in followed by George. Sheila's eyes light up clearly she is in love with Red.

SHEILA

Come in. Your Grandmother is in the kitchen.

DINNER TABLE

RED

I can't believe you married that man.

GEORGE

What have I done?

Ms. WAIT

George, you have been sweet.

GEORGE

I cannot do anything right with him.

RACHEL

This is only the first night together and already you are arguing.

Ms. WAIT

I deserve peace.

GEORGE

Red staying with us isn't going to work out.

SHEILA

Mom-Dad-Red can stay here.

RACHEL

(TO MS WAIT)

Elizabeth can move into Sheila's and Raina's room. You and George need peace.

Red

Okay. Thanks.

Sheila smiles.

INT. Villa-NIGHT

REDS ROOM

RED IS TALKING SWIGS FROM A BOTTLE OF WHISKY. HE STRUMS HIS GUITAR SLOWLY, STOPPING TO WRITE IN A NOTEBOOK. SHEILA ENTERS WEARING HER NIGHTGOWN.

SHEILA

Are you writing a song for me?

Sheila sits on the edge of Red's bed.

RED

I have been on the road for a long time. You shouldn't be in here dressed like that.

SHEILA

Will you kiss me?

SHEILA CLOSES HER EYES AND PUCKERS HER MOUTH.

RED

No. Go back to your bed.

INT. RAINA'S, SHEILA'S, AND ELIZABETH'S SHARED BEDROOM

RAINA AND ELIZABETH ARE STILL IN THEIR NIGHTGOWNS. RAINA IS PAINTING. ELIZABETH IS STILL IN BED. SHEILA IS SOUND ASLEEP.

ELIZABETH

Is there enough room for your easel?

RAINA

There is enough. Are you going to ballet?

ELIZABETH

What for? I dreamt about my father. He was planting a garden.
He looked up and said, I miss you, Elizabeth. The only time I
will see my father is in my dreams. I am staying in bed.

RACHEL

You finished college. You can sleep late and dream about your
dream job.

ELIZABETH

Father and I had plans to open a financial center together.
He said he would teach me great things and that I would own
and manage it. That is my dream job, but I can't foresee
owning and managing one with out my father. I will be working
alongside Heather-UGH-but it is the largest financial center
here-Goodnight.

RACHEL ENTERS THE ROOM.

RACHEL

Ballet class is starting.

ELIZABETH

I stopped going to ballet months ago.

Rachel

Sheila, Raina, please, leave the room.

RAINA CARRIES THE EASEL, CANVAS AND PAINT: SHEILA AND RAIN
LEAVE THE ROOM.

RACHEL

I have a surprise for you.

EXT. VILLA-DAY

YARD

RAINA CONTINUES TO PAINT ELIZABETH AND RACHEL HAVE DRIVEN
AWAY. RED SAUNTERS UP TO RACHEL AND LOOKS AT THE PAINTING.

RED

What is it?

RAINA

I don't know.

Red

That is what my band said about the songs I write-What is it?
It is feelings. All of us have them. You paint them-I sing
them.

RAINA PUTS HER HAND TO HER MOUTH TO SILENCE HER GIGGLES.

INT. Dance school - DAY

RACHEL AND ELIZABETH ARE SEATED. THERE ARE MANY YOUNG PEOPLE
SEATED AROUND THEM. THE DANCE SCHOOL AUDITORIUM IS FILLED TO
CAPACITY. ON THE STAGE AN ANNOUNCER ANNOUNCES TRYOUTS TO
ENTER A CONTEST.

(CLOSE UP ON POSTER)

THE GIN MODELING AGENCY IN THE UNITED STATES WILL CHOSE ONE
WINNER IN EACH CATEGORY OF RUNWAY AND ACTING. EACH WINNER
WILL WIN A CONTRACT WITH THE GIN AGENCY. THE WINNER WILL LIVE
AND WORK IN THE UNITED STATES.

ANNOUNCER

MY ASSISTANT IS PASSING OUT THE DIALOGUE FOR THE SKIT AND PASSING OUT THE NUMBER FOR THE ORDER IN WHICH YOU WILL BE CALLED. BRING THIS NUMBER TO THE STAGE WHEN YOUR NUMBER IS CALLED, SIGN THE RELEASE THAN WALK ACROSS THE STAGE TO THE TABLE AT THE FAR END. NUMBER ONE.

RACHEL

(WHISPERS TO ELIZABETH)

But YOU are number ONE.

ELIZABETH

(TO RACHEL)

Make that number two out of all these contestants-Winning this is TOO impossible.

ANNOUNCER

Number one.

Number One Contestant walks up the steps to the stage, she carries the number one card with her than hands it to the Announcer who in turn gives her a clipboard and pen. She writes briefly than strides elegantly across the stage to the table. There are two glasses of water on the table and two chairs under it. Contestant One looks at the dialogue than seats herself.

There is an actor standing at a table and two glasses of water.

ACTOR

We need to talk.

Both the actor and the contestant seat themselves.

Contestant one

About the other woman?

ACTOR

I am sorry.

Woman

I am too-but you will have to leave.

ANNOUNCER

Contestant number two.

Elizabeth holds the number two card in the direction of her mother. She walks up the steps onto the stage. The announcer hands Elizabeth a clipboard and a pen. She writes briefly than looks intensely at the dialogue. Vigorously, Elizabeth, walks across the stage than does a dancers leap, continuing her ballet walking in a dancers stride (chase (sha-SAY)) to the to the table where she stands.

ACTOR

Please, sit. We need to talk.

The actor moves the empty chair away from table and gestures for Elizabeth to sit.

Elizabeth

You sit. I talk.

The Actor sits.

If you are sorry, than act like a husband. Come home at night
Don't fool around with anyone, but me.

Elizabeth pours the glass of water over the actor'shead than
points her finger at him.

Laughter and clapping arise from the other Contestants. Some
of whom give a standing ovation.

INT. Rerald And Rachel's villa-night

KITCHEN

AT THE COUNTER, RAINA CHOPS A RED PEPPER. GERALD IS CHOPPING
AN ONION.

TABLE

(FOLLOW)

SHEILA IS BUSILY SETTING THE TABLE.

RED IS SEATED AT THE TABLE WITH A PENCIL IN HIS HAND,
WRITING.

SHEILA

What are you writing?

RED

A song. I have been inspired.

SHEILA

By me?

RED

Rain has inspired me.

SHEILA

It's not raining.

RED

Yes, it is.

ANGLE ON THE WINDOW

The yard is flooded with sunlight.

INT. GERALD'S AND RACHEL'S VILLA-NIGHT

RED'S BEDROOM

IN THE DARKNESS, SHEILA, WALKS THROUGH THE ROOM. RED IS
STRUMMING HIS GUITAR SOFTLY-WORKING ON A TUNE.

Red

Who is it?

SHEILA

It's Sheila. I have to talk to you about something.

Red

I am still working on this song, I can't talk right now. Go
back to bed.

EXT. GERALD'S AND RACHEL'S VILLA —MORNING (COND'T)

YARD

MS. WAIT IS IN HER NEIGHBORING YARD. RAINA IS OUTSIDE
PAINTING AT HER EASEL. RED BRINGS HIS GUITAR.

RED

Want to take a walk?

THEY HOLD HANDS AND WALK ACROSS THE YARD. RED SINGS.

RED (SINGING)

I met a girl with the rain in her name. Rain, rain, warm and
wet in a flowery dress. Sweet Caress. My Rain.

RAINA WITH HER EYES CAST DOWNWARD AND HER CHEEKS FLUSH, RUNS
INTO THE HOUSE.

(FOLLOW)

MS. WAIT CROSSES INTO THE YARD TO SPEAK TO HER GRANDSON, RED.

MS. WAIT

I didn't want to bother you while you were talking. I thought
we would see more of each other than we have.

RED

Aren't you busy with George?

MS. WAIT

George is my husband. Come, help me weed the garden.

INT. RESTAURANT - DAY

Elizabeth and Rachel are enjoying lunch. At a far corner
table a man is laughing with the five children of various
ages seated with him as he is feeding the youngest.

ELIZABETH

(To Rachel)

I do feel like there is hope.

HEATHER ENTERS THE RESTAURANT. SEEING THE MAN AT THE CORNER
TABLE WHO NOW IN KNELT ON THE FLOOR WIPING A STREAM OF MILK
THAT IS POURING OFF THE TABLE.

HEATHER

(ALOUD)

Hello Peter.

HEATHER SEEING RACHEL AND ELIZABETH, JOINS THEM FOR LUNCH.
RACHEL SMILES WHEN SHE RECOGNIZES THAT THE HAPPY MAN IS THE
PETER SHE KNEW FROM THE FINANCIAL CENTER.

INT. GERALD'S AND RACHEL'S VILLA-DAY

BEDROOM

ELIZABETH IS READING OLD E-MAILS FROM HER FATHER. WHEN HER
CELLPHONE RINGS.

ELIZABETH

Hello. I won.

ELIZABETH PUTS THE PHONE TO HER CHEST AND CALLS FOR RACHEL.

ElIZABETH

Mom.

Rachel hurries into her room. Elizabeth hands the cellphone to her mother.

ELIZABETH

It's the contest. Here, talk to them for me. This is too unbelievable.

SOON RACHEL ENDS THE CALL.

Rachel

You did win. You will be going to Los Angeles, California, USA to compete for the runway modeling contract with the Gin Agency.

ELIZABETH

I can take time off from the financial center.

RACHEL

The contest will pay for the trip for you and a plus-one.

ELIZABETH

Will you come with me, please.

RACHEL

Yes, sweetheart.

INT. GERALD'S AND RACHEL'S VILLA-DAY

Elizabeth and Rachel have their suitcases. They are dressed for the trip. Gerald hugs both good-bye. Raina stands beside Gerald. Sheila sits with her arms folded over her stomach.

GERLAD

(To Rachel)

I wish you didn't have to go.

RACHEL

(To Gerald)

It is only two weeks. I will call you every day.

RAINA

(TO ELIZABETH)

You are going to be the most beautiful.

SHEILA

I love you and I will miss you. Good-luck Elizabeth. Mom, when you get back I want to talk to you about something.

Rachel

Okay. Your Dad will be here.

Sheila

I know.

EXT. TOWN OF PEL-DAY

Raina and Red walk hand in hand. He carries an oversized guitar case over his left shoulder. Raina carries a large painting under her right arm. The stop in front of an apartment building.

RED

This would be a nice place to live

RAINA

Not in those unsightly apartments.

RED AND RAINA CONTINUE WALKING. THEY STOP IN FRONT OF THE UNIVERSITY.

RAINA

Red, aren't you coming in? I have to meet with the head of the art department than register.

RED

I'll stay. It is happening right here.

Red points to a radio station across the street, Pel Radio Broadcasting.

(PEL STREET (COND'T)

LATER

STILL CARRYING HER PAINTING, RAINA WALKS OFF THE UNIVERSITY CAMPUS ONTO THE SIDEWALK OF PEL STREET. SHE LOOKS AROUND FOR RED, THOUGH SHE CANNOT SEE HIM, SHE CAN HEAR HIM SINGING.

(ANGLE ON RED)

RED IS SITTING ON THE SIDEWALK WITH HIS BACK AGAINST A
BUILDING AND HIS GUITAR CASE OPEN. HE IS JUST ONE OF THE MANY
VENDORS AND ARTISTS ALONG PEL STREET. RAINA LOOKS BOTH WAYS
TWICE THAN CAREFULLY CROSSES THE STREET.

RAINA

What are you doing?

RED

(Singing)

I am singing. Making Money. Set your painting up beside me.

RED SETS DOWN THE GUITAR THAN PROPS RAINA'S PAINTING AGAINST
THE WALL. PEOPLE WILL STOP TO LOOK AND LISTEN. ONE SUCH
PERSON LINGERS IN FRONT OF RAINA'S PAINTING.

PERSON

I'll buy it.

EXT. GERALD'S/RACHEL'S VILLA-NIGHT

YARD

The moon is full. Raina and Red have their arms wrapped
around each other and are laughing hysterically. Once they
catch their breath, they kiss.

INT. GERALD'S AND RACHEL'S VILLA-NIGHT

Sheila is ill.

Sheila

My head is hurting. Will this ever go away?

GERALD

Here's your medication, lye down. I wish I could make you better. We'll pray.

LOS ANGELES, USA

INT. HOTEL-DAY

ROOM

RACHEL AND ELIZABETH SHARE A ROOM. RACHEL HOLDS OUT A RED CHIFFON DRESS THAT FLARES FROM THE HEM.

RACHEL

This is for you to wear to the judging.

INT. GERALD'S AND RACHEL'S VILLA-DAY

LIVING ROOM

GERALD IS SET A COOL CLOTH ON SHEILA'S FOREHEAD. HE THAN FOLDS HIS ARMS ACROSS HIS STOMACH.

LOS ANGELES, USA

Elizabeth's interview with Dawn D

DAWN D

I hope that you are enjoying your stay in L. A. If you pass this stage of the contest- the interview, you will meet Ronald and Gin -the owners of Gin Agency, at a lavish party where the final judging will take place.

There are no losers because you have already won a free trip to LA . Have you other travels you could tell me about?

Elizabeth slumps in the chair. She wipes her perspiring forehead with the back of her hand.

EliZABETH

My father liked to travel.

Elizabeth puts her hand to her face than walks out of the office.

INT. HOTEL ROOM-DAY (COND'T)

Rachel is still on the cellphone Elizabeth enters clearly distraught, throws herself across the bed.

RACHEL

(To Gerald)

I have to say good-night.

The call ends.

(To Elizabeth)

What happened?

ELiZABETH

(WEEPING)

I failed the interview. He started talking about traveling and I thought of my dad.

RACHEL

I am so sorry honey. I am sure you did fine.

ELIZABETH

I let you down.

Rachel

This wasn't for me.

RACHEL LAYS ACROSS HER OWN BED AND DOZES OFF TO SLEEP.

ELIZABETH THROWS HERSELF ACROSS HER BED BUT IS TROUBLED AND UNABLE TO SLEEP.

ANGLE ON

THE CRIMSON CHIFFON DRESS DRAPED ACROSS THE CHAIR.

ELIZABETH LOOKS UP DAWN D'S HOME ADDRESS ON HER SMART PHONE. SHE PUTS ON THE DRESS AND LEAVES WITHOUT PUTTING ON SHOES.

INT./EXT. DAWN D'SHOUSE-DAY(COND'T)

ELIZABETH STAND ON THE PORCH. DAWN D OPENS THE DOOR.

DAWN D

How in the world did you get my address?

EliZABETH

I have a good phone. Did I pass the interview?

DAWN D

You could have used it to call; but I am sorry-no. Good night-good morning-good-bye.

Dawn D closes the door, but Elizabeth catches it before it shuts. She follows Dawn D closely walking inside.

LIVING ROOM

Elizabeth stands, arms stretched out.

DAWN D

You are not my type.

Elizabeth dances while barefoot a beautiful dance.

DAWN D

The party is Tuesday.

FICTITIOUS COUNTRY

INT. GERALD'S AND RACHEL'S VILLA-DAY

RED'S BEDROOM

Raina and Red roll on the bed in an embrace.

Red kisses Raina.

INT. VILLA-DAY (COND'T)

DINING ROOM

GERALD SITS AT THE TABLE. A TALL GLASS OF MILK IS IN FRONT OF HIM. BESIDE HIM IS A BOWL INTO WHICH HE SPITS.

CLOSE-UP CRIMSON CONTENTS IN THE BOWL.

ANGLE ON GERALD'S EYES TEAR AS HE HOLDS HIS STOMACH.

LOS ANGELES, USA

INT. HOTEL-NIGHT

DANCE FLOOR WITH A RUNWAY -DAY

ELIZABETH WEARING THE RED CHIFFON DRESS MEET ALAN ROANALD'S
BROTHER. THEY WHIRL AROUND THE DANCE FLOOR WITH ALAN WHO IS
HANDSOME LIKE RONALD.

ALAN

A room full of people and I still do not get many dances.
Thank you for dancing with me.

RUNWAY

Ronald and Gin-the owners of the agency who are holding the
competition step onto the runway to speak to the contestants.

GIN

My husband, Ron and I congratulate you for being selected to
enter the runway division. Now, walk the runway. The music
will play, so when you get to the end, go dance. The winner
be announced.

The music begins. Contestants walk in a continuous stream
across the runway down and out to the dance floor. They dance
with one another. From the look on Elizabeth's face, she in
entranced by Ronald's good looks.

ElIZABETH

(To Alan)

Is Ronald a model.

Alan

No, my brother, he has never modeled. I think that you are the most beautiful contestant. I could put a word in with my brother and my sister-in-law in your favor.

ELIZABETH

No, thank you. You don't even know me.

ALAN

I would like to know you. Would you like to have dinner tomorrow.

ELIZABETH

That would be nice.

DISSOLVE TO:

INT. GERALD'S AND RACHEL'S VILLA-NIGHT

LIVING ROOM

RACHEL IS HOME AND HER SUITCASES ARE ON THE FLOOR GERALD AND RAINA HUG. SHEILA IS LAYING ON THE COUCH. RACHEL GOES OVER TO THE COUCH AND HUGS SHEILA.

RAINA

When will Elizabeth be back?

RACHEL

Elizabeth won the modeling contract so she should be back when the contract ends.

LOS ANGELES

INT. HOTEL DAY

RUNWAY

Models walk the runway.

ANGLE ON ALAN

ALAN IS BEHIND THE CURTAIN WITH ELIZABETH. HE IS COACHING
HER.

ELIZABETH

Distance, timing, step in slow rhythm and keep the arms close
to the sides.

AlAN

You are over analyzing. Elizabeth. Don't think of it as a
runway. Think of it as a fun-way.

RUNWAY

VARIOUS RUNWAY SHOWS

SHOW ONE

The models stop walking. Elizabeth bumps into the model in
front of her than falls back onto her bottom.

SHOW TWO

Each model walks to the edge of the runway, stop, turns than
walks. Elizabeth continues to walk off the end of the runway.

LOS ANGELES, USA

INT. RESTAURANT-NIGHT

TABLE

Alan, Ronald, Gin and Elizabeth are having dinner to discuss
Elizabeth's failed modeling.

GIN

Why do you think this is happening? Why are you not able to
do runway? You are a train ballet dancer.

RONALD

Elizabeth dances beautifully. What is happening?

AlAN

Clearly Elizabeth is nervous. Sweat pours from her forehead.

ELIZABETH

(To Alan)

Shut up.

INT. ALAN'S CAR NIGHT (COND'T)

Alan is driving Elizabeth home.

ELIZABETH

How dare you tell your brother and sister-in-law, my bosses,
I sweat.

AlAN

They can see you sweat.

ELIZABETH

Alan, you are not my husband.

ALAN

I wish that I were.

INT. GERALD'S AND RACHEL'S VILLA-DAY

Sheila is sick, laying on the couch. Rachel rubs Sheila's abdomen.

RACHEL

Your stomach is so hard. You will feel better after you menstruate.

SHEILA

I waited for you to get back; I wanted to tell you that I haven't had one in two months.

RACHEL

I will make an appointment with your doctor for you.

SHEILA

I am pregnant.

LIVING ROOM (COND'T)

Rachel confronts Red. Sheila, Raina and Gerald are in the room.

RACHEL

How could you take advantage of a sick girl.

RED

Ms. Ludwich, what did I do?

SHEILA

Mom, I am a woman, not a girl.

Rachel

You cannot take care of a baby.

GERLAD

Red, you proved that you are a real loser. You pig.

GERALD SWINGS HIS FIST AT RED HITTING HIM ON THE MOUTH, THUS KNOCKING HIM TO THE FLOOR. BLOOD TRICKLES OUT THE CORNER OF RED'S LIP.

RAINA

Daddy.

RACHEL

This should never have happened.

SHEILA

I am having Red's baby.

RED

Raina, let's get out of here.

RAINA

Yes Red, the apartment on Pel Street sounds good right now.

Raina looks at her mother, father, and Sheila than helps Red to his feet. Red and Raina leave.

A WEEK LATER

INT. SHEILA'S DOCTOR'S OFFICE-DAY

RACHEL AND SHEILA MEET WITH SHEILA'S DOCTOR.

SHEILA'S DOCTOR

Sheila, your exam shows you are not pregnant.

SHEILA

I had a dream that I was pregnant. When I missed my menstruation- I worried that it might be true. Red was in my dream, I went to ask him if it had really happened, but he was busy and didn't want to talk. Later, I was too embarrassed to ask him.

RACHEL

It's her medication. It doesn't help her pain but it makes her sleep a lot. In the daytime she is in a haze.

SHEILA'S DOCTOR

I think the medication has taken her appetite away. She is
sleeping and missing out on eating. This could have caused
the symptoms. She needs to eat more. I'll change her
medication.

INT. RON/GIN MODELING AGENCY-DAY

OFFICE

Elizabeth sits across from Ronald.

RONALD

You have fallen off runways; stepped on hemlines, ripping
expensive dresses; fallen off the runway and got a lump on
your forehead from walking into a door.

ELIZABETH

When I am dancing, it feels as if I am flying.

RONALD

Your contract stipulates that you must be able to perform the
duties of runway modeling. We have to quash your contract.

ELIZABETH

I have respect for the models. I adore the models. They are
good at what they do. This is not the career for me.

RONALD

Your work VISA will no longer be valid. We will pay for your ticket home.

ELIZABETH

Have you taken notice of all the financial centers here? Los Angeles is my home. This would have been a great area for my Father and I to open a financial center. I will open one to honor him.

INT. ALAN'S HOUSE- DAY

From the window can be seen another larger house.

ALAN

See over there. That's Ronald and Gin's house. We share the yard.

ELIZABETH

I am sorry I told you to shut up.

ALAN

I could never be mad at you. Do you want me to talk to my brother?

ELIZABETH

You would do that for me? You are a beautiful person. Do you still want to marry me?

ALAN

More than anything.

INT/EXT APARTMENT ON PEL STREET-DAY

RAINA AND RED HAVE MOVED IN TOGETHER. RAINA IS READING A BOOK FROM THE HANDBAG OF COLLEGE BOOKS. RED WALKS IN WITH HIS GUITAR OVER HIS SHOULDER. HE PEERS OUTSIDE THROUGH THE CURTAIN.

RED

Sheila is standing outside. She walked over to apologize. She doesn't look well. I tried to get her to come inside but she won't. It's beginning to rain.

RAINA GOES TO THE DOOR AND CALLS OUT TO SHEILA.

RAINA

Sheila, it's okay. Mom explained everything. It was just a misunderstanding.

Sheila enters holding her head. She falls to her knees.

INT./EXT. APARTMENT ON PEL STREET - DAY

DOOR

RACHEL SETS TWO HEAVY BAGS OF GROCERIES DOWN IN FRONT OF THE DOOR. RAINA, CARRYING A HANDBAG OF COLLEGE ART BOOKS WALKS UP BEHIND HER.

RACHEL

These bags are heavy.

RAINA

Thank you, mom. Come inside.

RACHEL

I have to go home to check on your father. He wasn't feeling well and than pick Sheila up.

Sheila's getting released from the hospital. They ran a brain scan on her, but they haven't found a reason for her headaches.

INT./EXT. GERALD'S AND RACHEL'S VILLA - DAY (COND'T)

RACHEL HEARS GERALD MOANING IN PAIN.

RACHEL

Gerald?

Rachel looks down to the floor at a puddle of blood. She rushes to her cellphone.

INT. HOSPITAL- DAY (COND'T)

Rachel stands in Gerald's hospital room; she is looking at the clock on the wall. Gerald's doctor enters.

RACHEL

I am supposed to pick my daughter up. I don't know what to do. She doesn't get better. Gerald doesn't get better.

DOCTOR

It is hard to see Gerald like this. We were study buddies in medical school. I wouldn't have made it through without him. Gerald has a stomach ulcer. The ulcerated part of his stomach should be removed.

RACHEL

Okay. Do it.

DOCTOR

I would like Gerald to have Robotic surgery.

Our country is slowly catching up to the rest of the world in
medical technology. I would like to arrange a medical
transport to the hospital in Los Angeles for his surgery.

RACHEL

We have a daughter who lives there.

EXT. PEL STREET -DAY

Red plays the guitar as people walk by. One particular
person, Yonnie, dressed finely, stops to listen.

Yonnie

(To Red)

Your sound is good. Stop by the radio station at seven
tonight. It's there, across the street. Upstairs to

The right is the Disk Jockey's Booth and I am D. J Yonnie.
Everybody needs time.

INT. APARTMENT ON PELL STREET-NIGHT (COND'T)

Red and Raina's dinner table is set. On it is a large roasted
turkey, bread, salad, milk and green beans.

Red walks through the door.

Where did the food come from.

RAINA

Mom came by. I was waiting for you.

RED

I don't have time to eat. I'm home to change my shoes. The D. J from the radio station told me to stop by.

RAINA'S CELLPHONE RINGS SOON AFTER RED LEAVES.

INT. SHEILA'S DOCTOR'S OFFICE-DAY

RACHEL

Sheila's father is going to Los Angeles for medical treatment. Could I get enough of her medication to last a couple weeks.

SHEILA'S DOCTOR

I don't see a tumor but we don't have the best diagnostics. I have Sheila sedated and on pain medication, but I can not keep Sheila's condition stabilized. Get her seen by a doctor while you are there. Take her medical records with you.

LOS ANGELES

A WEEK LATER

INT. LA HOSPITAL-DAY

Post-surgery. Elizabeth, Alan and Rachel stand watching as Gerald eats gelatin.

ELIZABETH

Gerald, when you are released, tomorrow, I want you, mom and Sheila to stay with us.

RACHEL

That is very sweet, thank you. I am going upstairs to see how Sheila is doing. They are prepping her for surgery.

GERALAD

Sheila and I are both on the surgical ward. She really is 'my' daughter.

INT. SHEILA'S DOCTORS OFFICE IN LA- DAY(CONDT)

Rachel is meeting with Sheila's surgeon.

SURGEON

We found her neck was damaged probably since birth which caused her ongoing headaches. It is good she was brought here and we can do surgery. She shouldn't have any more headaches.

Dissolve to:

EXT. ELIZABETH AND ALAN'S HOUSE-DAY

In the backyard, Rachel, Elizabeth, and Gerald sit outside. Alan is barbecuing.

RACHEL

Sheila is in rehabilitation to get her neck stronger. She will be wearing a neck brace for awhile when she gets released. The hospital social worker is helping Sheila, Gerald and I stay in the country and has found a teaching position at the local University for Gerald. We can't just marry someone like you did to stay here.

ELIZABETH

That was the plan, but plans change.

GERALD

Since I'll be teaching at the local university your mother can take classes there and Sheila can too for free.

RACHEL

The social worker said the university Gerald will be working at has a program to catch up on the studies Sheila had missed while she was ill. Than she can pick an area or study. I am going there too to study Viticulture. It is the study of growing grapes. I wish Rain were here: She would paint an interesting picture of the beautiful vineyards here.

ELIZABETH

Red is famous. What a break-discovered at a radio station.

RACHEL

He is touring.

GERALD

Things do get better.

RACHEL

I called Raina. She hasn't heard from Red and he hasn't deposited any money into their account.

GERALD

Don't worry about her, she is strong-she will be okay. We'll send her some money.

ELIZABETH

(To Gerald)

She is lucky she has the two of you. Mother mentioned that you two were going to take a second honeymoon now that you are healed. I have a gift for the both of you.

Elizabeth holds out two plane tickets.

ElIZABETH

The arrangements are made for your honeymoon. I also arranged
a side trip for you close to my father's crash site.

GERLAD

I thought it was a sailboat.

ELIZABETH

You will be flown to a small cabin near the site. In seven
hours, the plane will return to pick you up. It won't even be
a full day in the jungle. The small plane will drop you at
the airport where you than will fly to the honeymoon
destination.

RACHEL

Why?

Elizabeth points to a state of a Tasmanian Tiger.

ELIZABETH

For a memorial.

EXT/INT JUNGLE AREA -DAY

Rachel and Gerald experience a turbulent plane ride. The
plane circles several times before landing on a dirt runway.
The pilot points them in the direction of a small cabin.
Gerald picks up the one suitcase. Rachel and Gerald talk as
they walk towards the cabin.

GERALAD

What is this lump in our suitcase?

Rachel

It is the Tasmanian Tiger.

INT. SMALL CABIN-DAY

Gerald lays on a thin cot that is under the window. Rachel wipes cob webs away.

GERALAD

What was Elizabeth thinking about?

RACHEL

Her father.

GERALAD

I am going to sleep until the plane returns.

RACHEL

I am going to make John's memorial.

Gerald falls asleep. Rachel removes the Tasmanian Tiger Statue from the suitcase than carries it outside for several yards, finally dropping the heavy statue into place.

Two people approach Rachel. One points a gun at Rachel while the other, whose face is hidden by a large hat and a long beard, gathers small sticks.

PERSON WITH GUN

Check the cabin.

The bearded person runs several yards back to the cabin. He peers into the window which Gerald asleep under out of sight.

Rachel is led up a path to a wooden framed building. A tall fenced in area crowded with Tigers is near.

(Screams)

(The Tigers roar)

INT. WOOD FRAMED BUILDING DAY(COND'T)

The two brought Rachel to the Leader. The Leader refers to the bearded one as Blue Jay. Blue Jay's arms are full of small sticks.

The Leader

Blue Jay, pile the sticks in the corner.

Person one

(Holding the gun)

Found this wandering in the woods.

The Leader

What are you doing way out here?

RACHEL

I am on my second honeymoon.

THE LEADER

Here, for a honeymoon. No.

RACHEL

Could I get water, please.

THE LEADER

Blue Jay, bring water.

Blue Jay exits.

RACHEL

I'll be leaving in forty minutes when the plane comes back. I won't tell anyone. I don't care if you are growing drugs.

THE LEADER

Drugs are bad for people.

(OS tigers roaring)

The one referred to as 'Blue jay' enters carrying two cups of water. Blue Jay gives one to The Leader.

The other cup of water he gives to Rachel. Surprised to see that the one call Blue Jay is John with ears of beard growth, hair to his waist, and a vacant look on his face.

RACHEL

John.

The Leader

You know him?

RACHEL

I am a widow. Tomorrow would have been our wedding
anniversary. I came to make a memorial.

THE LEADER

You said second honeymoon. He has been here for years.

RACHEL

I didn't want you to know I was alone in the cabin.

THE LEADER

(To Rachel)

I was kind enough to put him to work after we pulled him from
the wreckage. He doesn't remember

His name but he can name every bird. So I call him Blue Jay,
for the first bird he named. He knows about tigers, too, but
his mind, he doesn't know the name of fruits. He doesn't know
what a rock is. Clearly, he doesn't remember you or he would
not have brought you to me. He follows orders with no

Question. Blue Jay is one of my best workers. Watch how well
he obeys. The plane will be back to pick her up, Blue Jay.
Take her back to the cabin-make it look like she's had a
fatal accident. We don't need outsiders knowing of our
operation.

John and Rachel walk along the path back towards the cabin.

Rachel

I told them we were married so they wouldn't know that Gerald is with me. Elizabeth opened a Financial center in the USA. I am supposed to tell you, not really tell 'you'. Do you remember me? What happened, John?

JOHN

The leader kept me working so much that he didn't realize my memory had returned. I hadn't recognize you when we came to see who the plane dropped off. My plane was shot down. I few too close to their operation.

RACHEL

We flew in fine.

JOHN

The locals know the flight path to stay clear of.

RACHEL

A 'Zoo' operation. I saw tigers.

JOHN

I thought it was a zoo. They are raising tigers for sale.

RACHEL

That is not a big deal, not enough to keep you prisoner or to kill me.

JOHN

This place operates by taking tiger body parts and making medicine from them. To increase virility, it is said, some people pay three hundred dollars for a bowl of tiger penis soup.

JOHN STOPS AT THE TASMANIAN TIGER STATUE, HE PICKS IT UP.

JOHN

The Tasmanian Tiger is considered extinct, but there has been sightings.

Small plane circles overhead.

RACHEL

It's the plane to take us out.

They begin to run.

EXT. CABIN- DAY(COND'T)

GERALD STANDS OUTSIDE LOOKING ABOUT FOR RACHEL. THE PLANE IS LANDED. THE PILOT HAS LOADED THE ONE SUITCASE. RACHEL AND JOHN RUN INTO VIEW.

GERLAD

Rachel!

RACHEL

We have another passenger.

PILOT

The plane cannot take too much extra weight.

JOHN

I'll stay.

THE PILOT OBSERVES JOHN THINNESS THAN TOSSES A TOOLBOX FROM
THE PLANE. JOHN LEAVES WITH THEM.

FICTITIOUS COUNTRY

INT. RAINA'S AND RED'S APARTMENT-DAY

Raina is typing an e-mail to her mother and her father.

(E-MAIL)

It is good to hear that Elizabeth's father has been found
alive-now she has her father back. He has been

Gone so long. Red is touring. He has been gone for six
months. My art isn't selling as it has been

Raining constantly and I cannot set them out for display and
places indoors want to charge a fee to use their space. I
have not signed up for classes. I used the school money you
sent for groceries and rent as I am still waiting for Red to
put money into our account. He isn't returning my messages.

ANGLE ON THE DOOR

RED WALKS IN CARRYING HIS SUITCASE. RAINA STOPS TYPING.

Raina

Six months with no call or e-mail from you, no word at all:
Our account is empty- What did you do 'party' all our money
away.

Red takes a diamond ring from his pocket.

Red

Will you marry me?

RAINA

Asking me when I am mad at you isn't romantic. Our bank account is empty. You never called me.

RED

I have been saving for the ring when I could. Food for the musicians and rooms we had to rent came out of my earnings. My cellphone got lost. I didn't get around to getting another one. I knew that your Mom and dad would get the things you needed.

RAINA

My dad got sick. My parents and both my sisters moved. I needed you. You were thinking about yourself.

RED

This is how it starts with disappointment than disaster.

Red picks up his suitcase than leaves.

INT. ms. Waits villa -day

Raina and Ms. Wait are having dinner.

Ms. WAIT

Raina, I called your parents. They have paid for a plane ticket for you. They want you joint them in the USA. Red came to see me and we talked.

RAINA

Is he coming back? He will because we love each other.

MS. WAIT

He left so you could live in peace. Peace is love.

INT. ALAN'S AND ELIZABETH'S HOUSE -DAY

Alan, Elizabeth, John, Rachel and Raina are sitting and conversing around the living room. They laugh. Raina sits in a chair in the corner smiling a shy smile.

RACHEL

We took sailing lessons. Our honeymoon was shortened after we found John so we figured a local honeymoon spent on the water is what we need.

ANGLE ON

Gerald and Sheila enter through the front door. They remove their shoes. Sheila, wearing a neck brace, puts down a small overnight bag than walks over to Raina. Sheila puts her arms around Raina.

SHEILA

I heard about Red-I am so sorry. Dad is teaching at the local college. You could take art classes again and start a life here.

Gerald

There is an opening at the college's advising office.

Angle on a painting hanging on the living room wall-signed by Raina.

FADE TO:

ESTABLISHING SHOT

THE CITY OF LOS ANGELES.

TWO BUILDINGS STAND OUT.

1. THE ELIZABETH'S FINANCIAL ADVISING/INVESTING BUILDING.

2. THE UNIVERSITY.

INT. UNIVERSITY-DAY

RAINA IS WORKING AT THE OFFICE COUNTER. SEVERAL STUDENTS ARE
SEATED IN THE WAITING AREA- BEHIND THEM HANG A PAINTING.

ANGLE ON A PAINTING OF A SAILBOAT-THE SAME PICTURE THAT RAINA
HAD SHOWN HER MOTHER WHO COMMENTED THAT SHE FEELS LIKE SHE IS
ON A VACATION WHEN SHE LOOKS AT IT, WHEN RAIN WAS A YOUTH. IT
IS SIGNED, RAINA.

LONG SHOT CALIFORNIA BAY

IN A SAILBOAT ON THE BAY, GERALD AND RACHEL TOAST WITH
GLASSES OF RED WINE. IT IS THE SAME SCENE AS IS IN RAINA'S
PAINTING.

GERALD

Things can get better.

Rachel holds her glass up.

RACHEL

Cheers to that.

They clink their glasses.

FADE OUT